I0622583

Jeremy Sullivan

Good Times Home

Full Circle: A Real Estate Journey in Poetry

YouAreAGoodPerson.com

Introduction

Welcome to this unique book, a journey through the multifaceted world of real estate encapsulated in short but meaningful poems. My name is Jeremy Sullivan, your guide, confidant, and fellow explorer in this adventure through properties and places, walls and windows, deals and dreams.

This book, "Good Times Home," is a comprehensive exploration into what it means to find a home, not just a structure of bricks and beams, but a sanctuary imbued with love, memories, and the vibrance of life. This poem, like others in this collection, aims to capture the essence of home, love, and the intricate life cycle we all navigate.

As a long-time resident of Baldwin County, Alabama, I bring a unique blend of local knowledge, experience, passion, and a dash of humor to the complex world of real estate. I am fully committed to pulling out all the stops for my client's satisfaction. I've been dubbed as having a "Good Times" reputation, and I strive to make every transaction successful and enjoyable. When work and passion collide, it's a beautiful thing, and for me, real estate is not just my job—it's my calling.

Whether you're an investor searching for hidden gems, a seller looking for the best deal, or a home buyer seeking that perfect place to call home, this book aims to touch your heart and inform your decisions. After all, real estate is more than just transactions; it's about making dreams come true.

So, as you turn these pages, you may find inspiration, insight, and perhaps a little piece of home.

to angie
my lover
you are the anchor
in my sea of chaos
you are the light
when darkness is boss
through each high and low
you stand beside
making me whole

to my family
your love
that lets dreams grow
you are the foundation
that never shakes

to my friends
you cheer and laugh
even when the world asks why
it's your presence
that makes the journey worthwhile

to my fellow real estate peers
each one a chapter
in my book of growth
from every encounter
I've taken an oath
to learn, to adapt
from lessons you've sown
both the good and the tough
have shaped the path I've known

Table of Contents

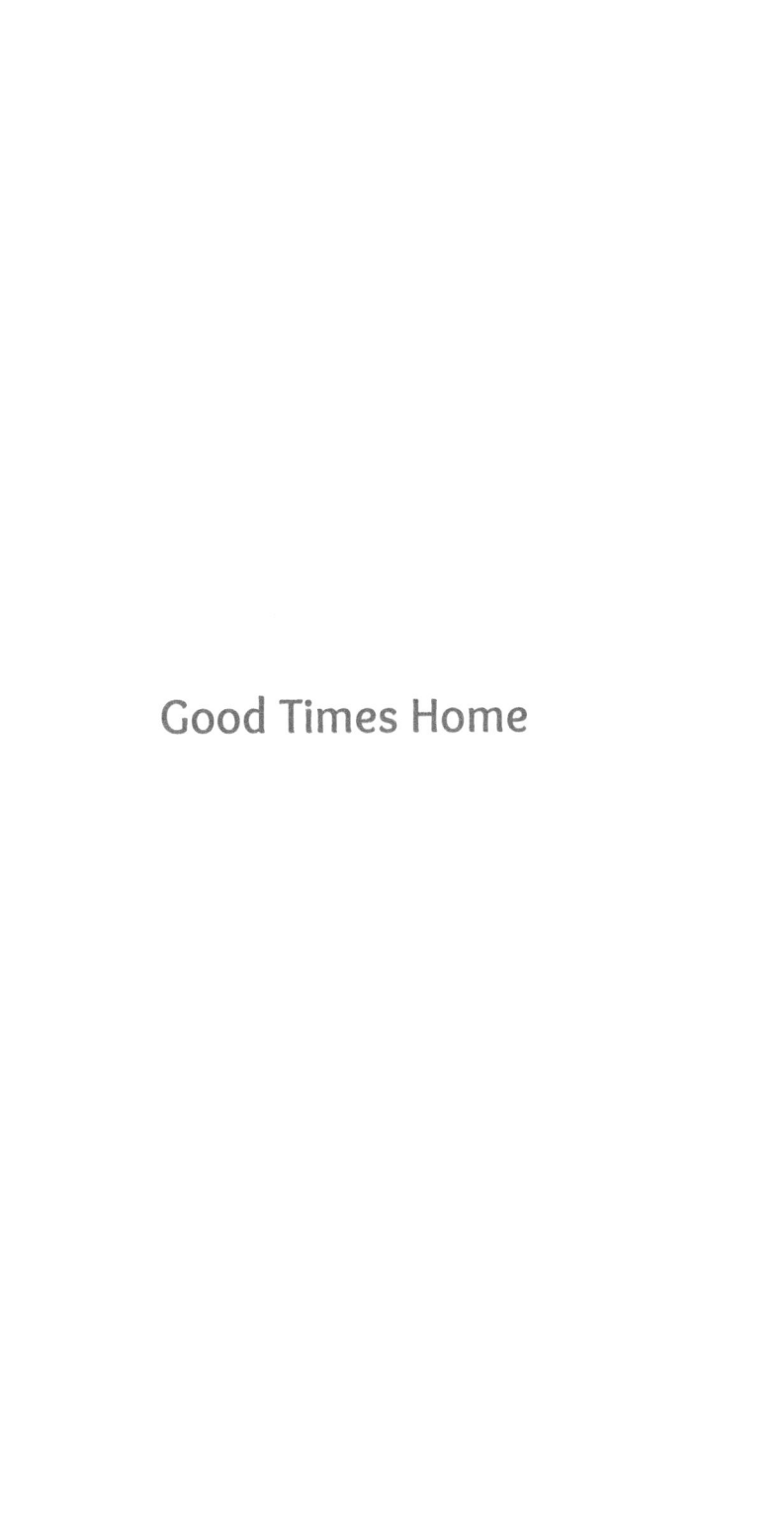

Good Times Home

house

it's only a house
a mere structure

walls are silent
corners quiet
but we know
when love moves in

walls start to whisper
our world
our place

it binds
our dreams
for a stage
where we play life

inside, outside too
in colors that mean so much

limitless paths together
an adventure
a promise

begin

agent

not just a guide
but a mirror
reflecting our hopes

the eyes
deep and knowing
not just seeing
but understanding

the handshake
firm yet warm
not just a greeting
but a pact

an oath taken
in papers and deals

not just transactions
but the weaving
of futures.

search

we sift
through listings

each one
a possibility

we step through doors
each an opening

to new potential
and adventure

a simple transition
from then to now

eyes wide
heart warms
big breath

this is
the one

agreement

the contract
not mere paper
but a map
to our dreams

the acceptance
our emotions
a happy pact

despite the odds
and others' opinions

the mortgage
a heavy word
yet lighter
with you

the closing
agreements and signatures
in harmony and accord
an adventure begins

the key
not just metal
but a promise
a symbol of home

home

four walls
and a roof
they say
it's just a house
but when love moves in
it becomes a home

the address
more than numbers
it's where
our heart resides

the driveway
not just a path
to the house
but to the heart

the porch
a threshold
between our peace
and the world's chaos

the lock
not for safety
but to treasure
what's inside

welcome

the door
it creaks
yet it speaks
welcome home

empty rooms
echoing
our future laughs
and whispers

the floor
beneath our feet
yet it holds
our world

the ceiling
not a limit
but a canvas
for our dreams

the fireplace
not as warm
as the love
that fills this place

the hallway
a passage
to new chapters
in our book

the closets
holds more than clothes
but our hidden selves
and other things
unseen on shelves

the bathroom mirror
reflects
not just our face
but truths

the attic
not just for things
we've forgotten
but for dreams
we'll rediscover

the stairs
each step
a journey
together

kitchen

where recipes
and memories
interlock

sounds and smells
weave twisted tales
in the heart's design

temperature meets touch
laughter fills the air
a comfort zone
where memories pair

standing
leaning
sitting
marking time

the heartbeat of the home

showpiece

the pool
reflecting
not just sun
but our joy

the lawn
green with envy
of the love
that lives here

the garden blooms
so do we
in this place
we call ours

the fence
not to keep out
but to cherish
what's within

the balcony
where we see
not just skies
but possibilities

the roof
shelters
not just people
but promises

evolution

moving boxes
filled with things
yet this space
is filled with feelings

we paint walls
and in each stroke
i find
a piece of us

we hang frames
but what we're really framing
is time

windows wide
letting in
not just light
but life

the curtains
they hide
not the view
but our sanctuary

the dining table
where we feast
not just on food
but on love

the sofa
where we rest
but never tire
of each other

the bed
a sanctuary
from the world
and into us

the pet
a witness
to our daily lives
and nightly dreams

the alarm
wakes us
to a new day
in our forever

the neighbors
not just next door
but in our lives

time

our home
where laughter echoed
and love was stitched
walls that witnessed
our highs and lows

rooms that held
our secrets close

but like seasons
we too must drift
from this cherished space

for every ending
we carry with us
the love and memories
that can't be replaced

this home
our home
where walls
whispered our joy

we loved
every laugh
every noise

it gave us
more than shelter
it held our voice

but like leaves
we must go

not goodbye

new dreams
carrying our love
to a new stage
where we play life

full circle

for sale sign
in the yard

is this
not an end
but a beginning

when the door
finally closes

walls are silent
corners are quiet

waiting to whisper
a new love
a new adventure
a new promise

we realize
not the end
but a beginning

Author's note

Dear Reader,

As you close this book, I hope you walk away with a newfound appreciation for the emotional and spiritual dimensions that real estate can offer. This collection of poems, led by "Good Times Home," aims to search into the deeper meanings of home, property, and the relationships that shape our lives.

Real estate is not just a profession for me; it's a passion deeply rooted in my identity. Being a long-time resident of South Baldwin County has granted me the privilege of discovering hidden gems in this beautiful locality, gems that I've tried to translate into words and share with you through this book.

You might have heard about my "Good Times" reputation. Well, I believe that life is too short for boring transactions. Whether buying, selling, or investing, the process should be as enjoyable as successful. That's the philosophy I bring into my real estate practice and the essence I've tried to capture in these poems.

My greatest joy is seeing my clients find their perfect home or property—where they can grow, love, and live. It's a joy that transcends the monetary aspect of real estate, touching upon the human need for belonging and happiness.

I often say work is play for me because real estate is more than just a job—it's a venue for making dreams come true.

Thank you for taking this journey with me. May your path to finding or creating a home be as fulfilling as it has been for me to guide you through these pages.

Good Times,

Jeremy Sullivan

Acknowledgments

Firstly, I would like to express my deepest gratitude to my wife, who has been a constant source of inspiration and support throughout this journey.

Awakening the Garden.

i was a garden
overgrown
with drought

you were the sun
that whispered
it's okay to bloom

I am also grateful to my friends and family for their unwavering support and encouragement.

A special thank you goes to Steven Shillito; his influence renewed my creative side and instilled the confidence to write this book.

To all my real estate colleagues, every encounter with you has been a learning experience for me.

I would also like to extend my gratitude to Rupi Kaur, whose expressive works have helped me connect with my emotions. The inspiration for the format of this poem owes much to her unique style.

YouAreAGoodPerson.com

Good Times

Copyright

© 2023 by Jeremy Sullivan. All rights reserved.
No part of this book may be reproduced in any form or by any electronic or
mechanical means, including information storage and retrieval systems, without
written permission from the author, except for the use of brief quotations in a
book review.

The ISBN is a unique identifier for this book title.
ISBN 979-8-9893015-0-8

GOOD TIMES HOME
Poems: Jeremy Sullivan
Editor-in-Chief: Jeremy Sullivan
Editors: Angie Sullivan, Stephen Shillito
Editorial Assistant: Jan Hicks, ChatGPT by OpenAI
Cover Photo: Canva Magic Switch
Cover: Jeremy Sullivan

www.ingramcontent.com/pod-product-compliance
Lightning Source LLC
Chambersburg PA
CBHW030528130626
46549CB00007B/3142